COOKING HEALTHY

COOKING WITH MEAT AND FISH

BY CLAIRE LLEWELLYN
WITH RECIPES BY CLARE O'SHEA

rosen publishing's
rosen central

New York

Published in 2012 by The Rosen Publishing Group Inc.
29 East 21st Street, New York, NY 10010

First Edition

Commissioning Editor: Jennifer Sanderson
Designer: www.rawshock.co.uk
Photographer: Andy Crawford
Illustrator: Ian Thompson
Hand Model: Camilla Lloyd
Proofreader and Indexer: Susie Brooks
Food Consultant: Clare O'Shea

Library of Congress Cataloging-in-Publication Data

Llewellyn, Claire.
Cooking with meat and fish / Claire Llewellyn, Clare O'Shea.
     p. cm. -- (Cooking healthy)
Includes index.
ISBN 978-1-4488-4845-4 (library binding)
1. Cooking (Meat)--Juvenile literature. 2. Cooking (Fish)--
Juvenile literature. 3. Cookbooks. I. O'Shea, Clare. II. Title.
TX749.L56 2012
641.6'6--dc22

                              2010039337

Manufactured in China
CPSIA Compliance Information: Batch #S11YA:
For Further Information contact Rosen Publishing, New York, New York at 1-800-237-9932

Photographs:

All photography by Andy Crawford, except: Alan & Sandy
Carey/Getty Images: COVER, 12; Nigel Cattlin/Alamy: 24; Peter
Dazeley/Getty Images: 40B; Natalie Forbes/Corbis: 38; Peter
Frischmuth/argus/Still Pictures: 31; Wayne Hutchinson/Alamy: 6;
iStockphoto.com: 8T & C, 13, 19, 25, 32, 40T Dave King/Getty
Images: 41; Lardi/Andia/Still Pictures: 9; Julian Love Photography/
Alamy: 4; PhotoEdit/Alamy: 30; Helene Rogers/Alamy: 11;
Visuals Unlimited/Corbis: 10

Note:

In preparation of this book, all due care has been exercised
with regard to the advice, activities, and techniques depicted.
The publishers regret that they can accept no liability for any
loss or injury sustained. Always follow manufacturers' advice
when using kitchen appliances and kitchen equipment.

Contents

Meat, Fish, and a Balanced Diet

Meat and fish appear on plates and menus in almost every part of the world. A wide range of animals are farmed or caught for their meat—from fish and shellfish to birds, such as chickens, and larger animals including pigs, cows, and sheep.

Doner kebab or shawarma, a Turkish specialty, is made of layered slices of lamb, cooked on a vertical spit. The sliced meat is added to pita bread with pickles, salad, and a yogurt sauce.

Food and Culture

The food we eat, or our diet, is influenced by many things, such as whether we live in a hot or cold climate, in the mountains, or by the sea. For example, people who live in coastal regions often eat more fish and seafood, because it is more readily available than meat and chicken. People's diet also depends on their culture and beliefs. Meat and fish are often the core part of a meal—but many people are vegetarians and choose not to eat these products. The way we prepare and eat any food can be an important part of tradition, featuring in family events, national dishes, festivals, and ceremonies that vary around the world.

A Healthy Diet

Our diet is an important part of a healthy lifestyle. There are five main food groups that contain different nutrients that work together to keep the body healthy. These groups are often shown on a "food plate," where you can see the proportions in which they should be eaten (see page 5). Added to these food groups is water. We need about six to eight glasses of water each day to keep our bodies healthy.

Meat, poultry, fish, and shellfish are excellent forms of protein. Eggs are another protein-rich food, along with plant foods such as legumes, nuts, and seeds.

The Food Plate

Fruit and vegetables: Full of vitamins and minerals, these foods protect our body and reduce the risk of heart disease, stroke, and some cancers. The fiber in them helps to bulk up our food and keep our digestive system healthy. Fruit and vegetables are low in fat, so they fill us up without unnecessary calories.

Carbohydrates: These provide us with energy. Starchy carbohydrates, which include grains and cereals, should make up about 30 percent of the food we eat. Starchy carbohydrates are an important source of energy for sportsmen and women because they release the energy slowly, keeping the body going for longer.

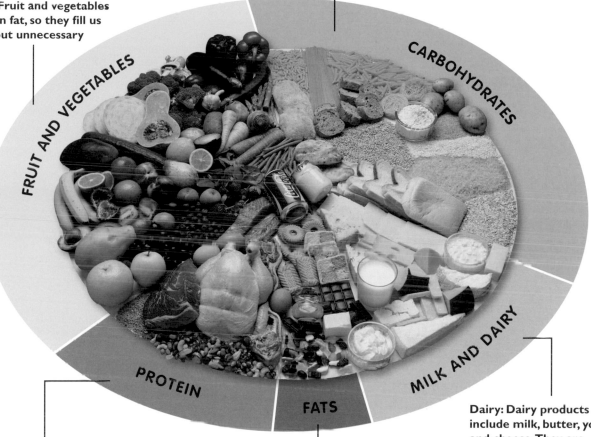

Protein: This builds and repairs our bones, muscles, skin, hair, and tissues. Meat, fish, eggs, and legumes that provide body-building proteins should make up about 15 percent of our total daily diet.

Fats: These keep us warm and can also be stored in the body for energy. Foods that are high in saturated fats (fats from animal sources) or sugar, such as cakes, cookies, and chips, should be eaten only in small amounts (about 8 percent of our total diet). Fats found in oily fish, olives, and nuts and seeds are called unsaturated fats. Saturated fats are linked to an increased risk of heart disease. Eating unsaturated fats is a healthier alternative.

Dairy: Dairy products include milk, butter, yogurt, and cheese. They are packed with nutrients, such as calcium, magnesium, Vitamin K, zinc, and protein, and help to build strong bones and teeth. Yogurt is full of good bacteria and improves our immune system and digestive health. It is best to eat cheese in moderation because it is high in fat.

FOOD FACTS

Eating a moderate amount of protein, in one or two meals every day, will give you all the protein you need for a balanced diet. Here are some examples of a moderate serving of protein:

2–3.5 oz. (60–100 g) boneless meat or poultry
3.5 oz. (100 g) fish
2 medium eggs
3 tablespoons of seeds
3 tablespoons of nuts

Looking at Meat and Poultry

Meat and poultry are tasty, nutritious foods that are easy to prepare. With their different flavors and cuts, they are very versatile and provide us with a lot of choice.

Which Meats?

The most popular meats are beef (from cows), lamb (from sheep), and pork (from pigs). These are all known as red meats. Poultry refers to farmyard birds such as chicken and turkey, and these birds produce white meats. Other edible birds include duck, pheasant, Cornish game hen, and goose. Veal (from calves), venison (from deer), rabbit, and hare are also eaten.

 In summer, cattle raised for their beef graze on grass. In the late fall, they are taken inside and fed on grains and silage (conserved grass).

Meat in the Diet

Meat and poultry are high in protein, which helps the body to grow and repair itself after injury. These foods are also a good source of vitamins and minerals, especially iron. Iron is important for the body, helping it to form the red blood cells that carry oxygen to every organ. Some cuts of meat can be high in fat, so it is wise to choose leaner cuts and remove any visible fat. The meat from poultry is a good choice because it is lower in fat.

Organ Meats

While the word "meat'" refers to an animal's muscle tissue, the term "organ meats" is the name given to any other part of its body. Well-known examples of organ meats include the brain, liver, kidneys, and tongue. Organ meats are rich in iron and vitamins, but they have a strong flavor and are less popular today than in the past. However, they are still often combined with other meats—for instance, in patés.

How Was It Farmed?

Meat and poultry may be farmed intensively indoors or "free range" outdoors. Some people have complained about the conditions on intensive farms. Whatever its source, all meat is equally nutritious. Check the label to find out how the meat you have bought has been farmed. The label should also tell you if the product is organic, or free from chemical preservatives.

Processing Meat

Fresh meat and poultry can be ground up and mixed with other ingredients to make sausages, patés, and pot pies.

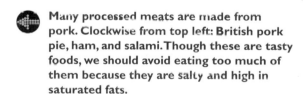

FOOD FACTS

We do not need a lot of meat in our daily diet. About 2–3.5 oz. (60–100 g) per day is sufficient, eaten with plenty of vegetables and starchy foods, such as rice, noodles, or potatoes.

Meat can also be cured to make salami-type sausages, bacon, ham, and other processed meats. We should avoid eating too many processed meats because they are high in saturated fats and contain a lot of salt. Too much salt increases the risk of a heart attack or stroke.

What About Vegetarians?

Many people choose not to eat meat for religious, ethical, or dietary reasons. So where do they find their daily protein? Cheese is high in protein but also high in fat. A better choice are the plant proteins, which include different types of legumes as well as nuts and seeds. Legumes must be combined with grains, seeds, or nuts to provide a complete form of protein—for example, in the meal of baked beans on toast. These, combined with eggs, dairy products, cereals, and rice, will provide all the protein the body needs.

Many processed meats are made from pork. Clockwise from top left: British pork pie, ham, and salami. Though these are tasty foods, we should avoid eating too much of them because they are salty and high in saturated fats.

It is much healthier to eat lean meat and poultry instead of processed meat. When cooking meat and poultry, cut off any visible fat before you cook it.

Looking at Fish

From haddock to halibut and pollock to sole, fish is delicious, healthy, and cooks very quickly.

Fish in the Diet

Fish is such a healthy food that nutritionists recommend that we try to eat it twice a week. Fish is low in fat, a great source of protein, and contains many vitamins and minerals.

Some kinds of fish are more nutritious than others. Oily fish, such as mackerel and trout, contain oils known as Omega-3 oils. These unsaturated fats help us to think and use our brains well, and lower the risk of heart attacks.

Which Fish?

Fish can be sorted into three different groups:

Variety	Fish
Oily fish	Tuna, trout, sardines, mackerel, salmon, herring, and fresh tuna are known as oily fish. Oily fish are very healthy because they contain Omega-3 oils.
White fish	Cod, haddock, sole, and flounder are among the best-known white fish. They have a delicate flavor and are very low in fat.
Shellfish and other seafood	Shrimp, mussels, crabs, and lobster are known as shellfish. They contain similar nutrients to white fish and are rich in minerals. Squid (and its cousin, the octopus) is a kind of mollusk. This seafood can be used in many dishes and is high in protein.

FOOD FACTS

The Japanese eat more fish than any other country. Japan has one of the lowest levels of heart disease in the world.

 Mussel farming is a natural process. Baby mussels attach themselves to ropes or poles, take in food as they need it from the water, and are harvested after three years when they are fully grown.

Finding Fish

Fish is the world's last great wild food resource. Most of the fish we buy in the shops has been caught in seas and oceans. However, fish stocks are declining, and an increasing amount of certain species, such as salmon, trout, shrimp, and mussels, are now raised on fish farms. This is known as aquaculture. Fish on fish farms are fed regularly, so they do not have to swim to hunt for food. Due to this lack of exercise, farmed fish have a layer of fat.

Processing Fish

Fresh fish is combined with other ingredients to make fish fingers, fish cakes, patés, soups, and pies. Fresh fish spoils easily, so much of it is preserved by freezing, drying, salting, or smoking. Smoked fish includes smoked herrings, smoked salmon, smoked trout, and smoked mackerel. Fish such as tuna, mackerel, and crab meat can also be preserved in brine, oils, or water, and canned. Seafood, such as mussels, can be preserved and sold in bottles or jars.

 Smoked mackerel (left) and canned tuna (right) are two kinds of processed fish. The mackerel contains oils that are good for our health. While fresh tuna also contains these oils, canned tuna does not. This is because the fish is cooked before the canning process.

Before you start to cook with meat or fish, it is important to know about keeping it fresh and safe to eat. Like most foods, meat and fish contain bacteria that can become harmful if you are careless.

Beating Bacteria

There are two main types of bacteria—one that makes the food spoil or rot, and one that can cause food poisoning and make you sick. Salmonella, listeria, and *E. coli* are just some of the dangerous bacteria you might have heard of. These are examples of bacteria that cause food poisoning. Fortunately, it is easy to destroy these bugs, or stop them from spreading, by storing food at the right temperature, handling it carefully, and cooking it in the correct way.

FOOD FACTS

It is not always easy to tell if food is contaminated because often it looks, smells, and tastes fine. Symptoms of food poisoning include fever, vomiting, stomach pains, and diarrhea.

Sensible Storage

Bacteria thrive at room temperature, so place well-wrapped meat and fish in the refrigerator or freezer as soon as you return from the store. Store raw meat and fish at the bottom of a refrigerator, away from cooked foods, cheese, and vegetables, to avoid contamination.

 Handle with care! A greatly magnified view of *E. coli* bacteria, which can cause food poisoning.

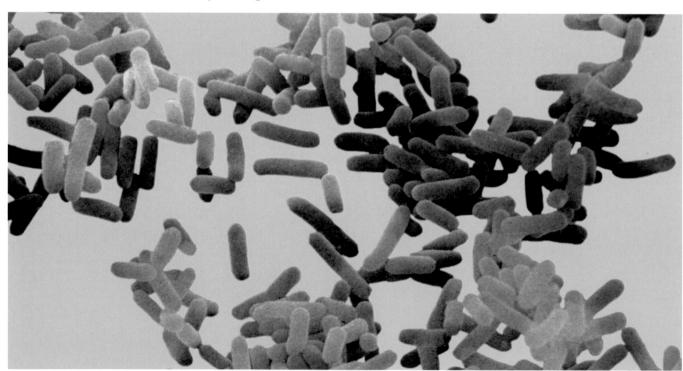

Food	Storage time in a refrigerator
Raw fish	1 day
Raw meat	2 days
Raw poultry	2 days
Raw organ meats	1 day
Raw sausages	3 days
Cooked meats	2 days

Careful Cooking

Make sure you cook meat and fish thoroughly—it should be searing hot all the way through. With poultry, ground meat, and sausages, make sure there is no pink left on the inside. When these meats are fully cooked, the juices should run clear.

Leftovers

If you have cooked meat or fish and are not going to eat it right away, cool it as quickly as possible and then put it in the refrigerator or freezer. When you reheat it, make sure it is steaming hot.

Defrosting Frozen Meat and Fish

When meat or fish thaws, a lot of liquid may come out of it. This liquid will spread bacteria onto any food, plate, or surface that it touches. Keep meat or fish in a sealed container, preferably at the bottom of the refrigerator, so that it cannot touch or drip onto other foods. Do not leave it at room temperature, where bacteria will multiply.

If you defrost raw meat or fish and then cook it thoroughly, you can freeze it again—but never reheat foods more than once.

Handling Raw Foods

Always thoroughly clean plates, utensils, work surfaces, and your hands after they have touched raw or thawing meat or fish. This will stop harmful bacteria from spreading. Never let raw meat come into contact with cooked food, or ready-to-eat raw food such as salad vegetables—the bacteria will not be destroyed if the food is not going to be cooked further and could cause food poisoning. Use separate cutting boards for raw meat, poultry, and fish.

 To keep food safe, refrigerate! Food should not be left out for more than an hour. Put meat and fish in the refrigerator as soon as you get it home.

Beef is a dark, nutritious red meat with a deep, rich flavor. It can be used in a huge variety of dishes, including roasts, warming stews, meat pies, and spaghetti bolognese.

Raising Beef Cattle

Beef cattle are reared all over the world, but especially in places where there is plenty of grazing, such as Australia, Brazil, Argentina, and Canada. Most breeds of beef cattle are different from the breeds used for milk. For generations, beef cattle have been bred to grow quickly, producing a lot of meat. They mostly graze in fields during the summer and are kept indoors in the winter when the grass has stopped growing. Then they are fed on dried or preserved grass, supplemented with grains or beans. Beef cattle are slaughtered when they are about 18 months old. After slaughter, the animal is hung for between one and three weeks to give the meat a fuller flavor.

 Some beef farmers rear cattle from birth to slaughter. Others sell their animals on for fattening after 6 to 12 months.

Veal

Veal is the meat of young male dairy cows, which cannot produce milk. It was once unpopular because of poor farm practices, but today, this meat is being raised to high welfare standards in many countries, such as the UK. All British animals live outdoors in the summer and feed on natural food. The animals go to slaughter when they are five months old. The tender pink meat is delicately flavored and contains virtually no fat. Like beef, veal can be roasted or stewed. The best meat is cut into slices and beaten thin to make escalopes. Wiener schnitzel, a well-known Austrian dish, uses escalopes of veal.

Processing Beef

Beef is processed in many different ways. The fresh meat can be ground and made into beef burgers or chopped and added to stews and pies. Beef can also be preserved by salting or curing to produce bresaola, pastrami, or corned beef, which are sold at the delicatessen counter.

Who Eats Beef?

Beef is eaten in most parts of the world. The UK is famous for its roast beef served with Yorkshire pudding, while steaks and hamburgers are devoured in North and South America and Australia. Beef is not popular in India, where the cow is sacred to the Hindu religion, or in the Middle East, where people traditionally prefer lamb.

 Beef burgers are served in a soft bun with a choice of extras, such as lettuce, tomato, onion, pickle, a slice of cheese, mustard, ketchup, mayonnaise, salsa, and peppers.

FOOD FACTS

Beef burgers are also known as "hamburgers." The name comes from the German city of Hamburg, where sandwiches of hot ground beef used to be very popular. Hamburgers never contain ham!

Cuts of Beef

A beef animal's carcass is quartered and cut into various pieces. Each part produces different meat that needs cooking in different ways (see below). Some of the tougher cuts may be put through a grinder. Ground beef is very versatile and can be used in many dishes including meatballs, beef burgers, bolognese sauce, or spicy chili con carne.

Ribs: These prime cuts are great for roasting. The ribs are marbled with fat and are the most flavorful.

Steaks: Tenderloin, sirloin, and T-bone steaks are some of the tenderest, leanest cuts of beef. They are suitable for broiling or frying, or slicing up in stir-fries.

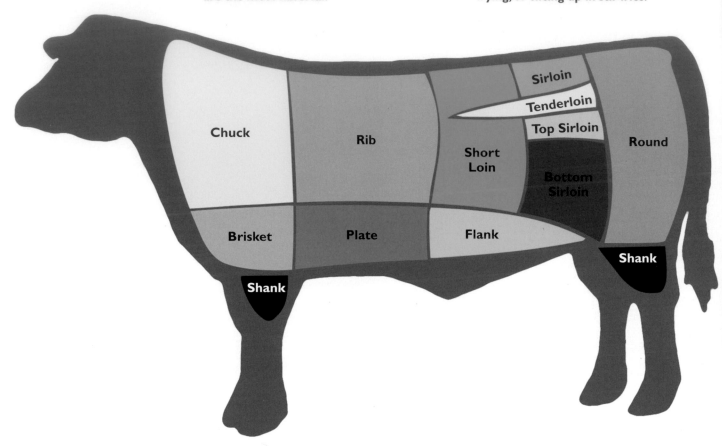

Brisket, shank, plate, flank: These cuts are cheap and tasty but tend to be tough. They are suitable for long, slow cooking in stews and casseroles.

Round steak: This cut is lean but can be tough. It is best cooked slowly using moist heat and is suitable for braising or pot-roasting.

KNOW YOUR FOOD

Fresh beef has cream-colored fat and bright red meat. Choose well-trimmed, lean cuts of meat without too much fat. If buying ground meat, check the fat content and choose the lowest amount for the healthiest option.

Cooking Beef

Cooking beef, and other types of meat, makes it more tender and digestible. In addition to cooking, there are various methods to ensure the meat is perfectly prepared before eating. These techniques can be used for other types of meat, too.

FOOD FACTS

Marinating is the process of soaking foods in a seasoned liquid. The ingredients for marinades come from three groups—acids, oils, and seasonings. Acids, such as fruit juice or vinegar, will tenderize meat. Oils lock in its flavor and moisture. Seasonings, such as herbs and garlic, add flavors.

Technique		Description
	Trimming	Trim any fat off the edge of the beef before cooking it so that the cut is leaner and more healthy.
	Scoring	If you score the meat before you marinate it, the marinade will be able to soak right into the cut.
	Marinating	The longer meat is left to soak up the marinade, the more flavorful and tender it will be (see below).

Beef Marinade

SERVES: 2   **PREPARATION TIME: 10 MINUTES**   **COOKING TIME: NO COOKING**

If you leave meat overnight in this marinade, it will be lovely and tender when you come to cook it.

Ingredients:
1 garlic clove
1 tablespoon soy sauce
juice 1 lime

1. Peel and crush the garlic.

2. Combine the crushed garlic, soy sauce, and lime juice.

3. Pour liquid over the meat you want to marinate. If possible, allow the meat to marinate overnight in a sealed container in the refrigerator.

Lasagna

Lasagna is a traditional Italian al forno pasta dish. *Al forno* means "from the oven."

Ingredients

3.5 oz. (100 g) Cheddar cheese, grated
1 tablespoon all-purpose flour
2¼ cups (500 ml) milk
1 tablespoon vegetable oil
½ lb. (225 g) ground beef
2 garlic cloves, peeled and finely chopped
1 onion, peeled and chopped
14 oz. (400 g) can tomatoes
1 tablespoon tomato purée
½ teaspoon sugar
1 beef stock cube
5 oz. (150 g) dried lasagna sheets

1. Preheat the oven to 400°F (200°C).

2. To make the cheese sauce, place three-quarters of the Cheddar cheese, plus the flour and milk, in a saucepan over medium heat. Stir continuously in a figure eight until the sauce thickens. Remove from the heat.

3. To make the meat sauce, heat the oil over medium heat and fry the beef, garlic, and onion until the meat has turned brown and the onions are soft. There should be no pink on the meat.

4. Add the chopped tomatoes, tomato purée, and sugar to the meat. Crumble the stock cube into the meat sauce and stir well.

5. Heat the sauce to boiling then turn off the heat.

6. To assemble the lasagna, start with a layer of meat sauce, then a layer of lasagna sheets and some cheese sauce. Repeat until all the meat sauce, pasta, and cheese sauce is used up, finishing with a layer of cheese sauce.

7. Sprinkle the remaining cheese on top and bake in the oven for 30 minutes until golden brown.

COOK'S TIP

Try using a mixture of cheeses, such as Parmesan and Cheddar.

Burgers

SERVES: 2 | **PREPARATION TIME: 20 MINUTES** | **COOKING TIME: 10–12 MINUTES**

Originally hamburgers were from Hamburg in Germany. Their popularity has spread and today, people all over the world eat burgers.

Ingredients

11 oz. (300 g) ground beef
1 small onion, peeled and chopped
salt and pepper
1 egg
1 tablespoon soy sauce
2 soft hamburger buns
mayonnaise (optional)
ketchup (optional)
1 medium tomato, sliced
6 slices cucumber
4 iceberg lettuce leaves
french fries, to serve

1. Put the ground beef, onion, salt, pepper, egg, and soy sauce in a bowl and squeeze it together using your fingers.

2. Divide the meat mixture into four equal portions and pat firmly into round burgers.

3. Turn the broiler on high and broil the burgers for 6 minutes on each side.

4. In the meantime, prepare the buns. Cut each bun in half and spread mayonnaise to taste on the bottom and ketchup to taste on the top.

5. Add 2 leaves of lettuce, some tomato slices, and 3 slices of cucumber to each bun.

6. When the burgers are cooked, add them to the buns. Serve immediately with french fries.

Beef and Pepper Stir-Fry

SERVES: 4 | **PREPARATION TIME: 20 MINUTES** | **COOKING TIME: 15 MINUTES**

Piping hot stir-fries are tasty to eat and quick and easy to make.

Ingredients

11 oz. (300 g) lean beef
1 garlic clove, peeled and finely chopped
1 tablespoon vegetable oil
1 red pepper
5 bok choi leaves
¾ cup (200 ml) oyster or soy sauce
2 packages instant noodles
2 tablespoons cold water

1. Slice the beef into strips about ½ in. (1 cm) wide.

2. Put the beef and garlic into a wok or large frying pan with the oil and set aside.

3. Deseed and slice the red pepper into strips, about ¼ in. (5 mm) wide. Slice the bok choi into strips about ½ in. (1 cm) wide.

4. Fry the beef and garlic over medium heat until there is no pink left on the meat.

5. Add the oyster sauce and stir well.

6. Add the peppers and bok choi and cook for 5 minutes, stirring all the time.

7. Add the noodles and water and cook for another 5 minutes. Serve piping hot.

Lamb

Lamb is a tender, delicious red meat that is eaten all over the world. It is ideal for a variety of dishes, including barbecued kebabs, roasts, and stews.

Breeding Sheep

Sheep are hardy animals. They can be kept outdoors for much of the year, grazing on rough ground. Breeds are chosen to suit the climate and land—for example, tough, sure-footed sheep are selected for places with a harsh climate and rugged terrain. The sheep are often allowed to roam over large areas so that they can find enough food to survive. In many upland areas, they are brought down into valleys in the winter, for protection from the bitter weather. On better grassland, sheep have been crossbred, resulting in animals with useful characteristics. They are strong, look after their young, and give birth to plenty of fast-growing lambs that provide excellent quality meat.

Rearing Lambs

Most lambs are born in early spring when the grass is starting to grow. They suckle from their mothers at first, then gradually begin feeding on pasture or hay and cereal feed. The young

Exporters

Producers

 This map shows the main producers and exporters of lamb.

 Lamb tagine is a tasty, slow-cooked dish from Morocco. The word "tagine" refers to the cone-shaped cooking dish in which the stew is cooked.

animals are separated from their mothers when they are four months old. They go to slaughter throughout the summer. The younger the animal, the more tender its meat.

Who Eats Lamb?

Lamb is a familiar meat in most parts of the world. In Greece, a whole lamb is roasted very slowly to make a popular dish called kleftiko. Lamb is also ground and combined with eggplant to make the dish moussaka.

In North Africa, lamb tagines are made from stewed lamb and are often served with couscous (a grainy dish made from crushed wheat), while lamb kebabs are popular throughout the Middle East. The Indians add lamb to curries, and it also forms the base to traditional British dishes such as Lancashire hot-pot and shepherd's pie.

Lamb is cooked as part of a traditional Easter Sunday dinner in many families, including those living in the United States. A leg of lamb may be roasted and served with vegetables such as carrots, green beans, and potatoes.

FOOD FACTS

Some shepherds keep mixed flocks of sheep and goats. Goat is eaten instead of lamb in parts of Europe, Central and South America, Pakistan, India, and the Far East. Curried goat is popular in Jamaica.

Cuts of Lamb

Lamb is a red meat, though the younger the animal, the paler its meat. The carcass is cut into various pieces, which need to be prepared in different ways. Some cuts, such as the leg, can be roasted, while chops can be quickly broiled or fried. Other cuts, such as lamb shank, need many hours of slow cooking until the meat is meltingly tender and almost falling off the bone. Ground lamb is delicately flavored and can be used in dozens or ways—for example, to make meatballs or in a stuffing for bell peppers or other vegetables.

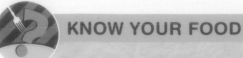

KNOW YOUR FOOD

Choose well-trimmed, lean cuts of meat without too much fat. Lamb meat should be pink, and its fat should be firm and creamy white. If you are buying ground lamb, check the fat content and go for the lowest amount.

Loin chops and rack: Chops are cut from the loin. Cutlets come from the rack. These pieces of meat on the bone are useful to serve as individual portions. They are tender and tasty when broiled, fried, or barbecued.

Leg of lamb: Juicy and flavorful, this cut is suitable for roasting. The tender meat can also be cut from the bone and diced for kebabs and stir-fries. Leg of lamb is often served with mint sauce or jelly to bring out the flavor.

Shoulder: A flavorful though rather fatty joint, this is suitable for roasting and will feed a large number of people.

Shoulder

Rack

Loin

Leg

Foreshank

Breast

Flank

Hindshank

Shanks: These cheaper cuts of meat are best slow roasted or in stews and casseroles, when the meat becomes very tender. This meat is also used to make ground lamb.

Moussaka

SERVES: 2 | **PREPARATION TIME: 30 MINUTES** | **COOKING TIME: 30 MINUTES**

Moussaka is a traditional Greek dish of ground lamb, eggplant, and a cheese sauce.

Ingredients
1 large eggplant, stem removed and sliced
salt
4 tablespoons olive oil
14 oz. (400 g) ground lamb
1 onion, peeled and finely chopped
2 garlic cloves, peeled and finely chopped
14 oz. (400 g) can tomatoes
1 tablespoon tomato purée
1 teaspoon dried oregano
1 beef stock cube
2 oz. (50 g) grated Cheddar cheese
1 cup (250 ml) milk
1 tablespoon flour
Greek salad, to serve

1. Preheat the oven to 350°F (180°C).

2. Sprinkle salt onto the eggplant slices and allow them to stand for 15 minutes. Rinse them under cold running water and pat dry with paper towel.

3. Heat one-third of the oil in a frying pan over medium heat and fry one-third of the eggplant until slightly brown. Repeat until all the eggplant pieces are done. Set them aside until later.

4. Fry the lamb, onion, and garlic until brown. Add the tomatoes, tomato purée, oregano, and the stock cube. Stir well and heat to boiling. Allow to simmer for about 20 minutes.

5. In the meantime, make the cheese sauce. Put the cheese, milk, and flour into a saucepan and stir constantly in a figure eight over medium heat until the sauce thickens.

6. Put the meat sauce in a large ovenproof dish, lay the fried eggplant slices on top, and cover with the cheese sauce.

7. Bake for 30 minutes. When ready, cut into portions and serve with Greek salad.

COOK'S TIP

To make a Greek salad, combine cucumber slices, cherry tomatoes, feta cheese, and black olives. Drizzle with olive oil.

Shepherd's Pie

This English lamb dish is sometimes cooked with ground beef and called cottage pie.

Ingredients
4 medium potatoes
1 tablespoon vegetable oil
7 oz. (200 g) ground lamb
1 small onion, peeled and
  finely chopped
14 oz. (400 g) can vegetable soup
3 tablespoons milk
1 tablespoon butter
2 oz. (50 g) Cheddar cheese, grated

1. Preheat the oven to 350°F (180°C).

2. To make the mashed potato, half fill a medium-sized saucepan with water and place it over medium heat to boil. Peel and cut each potato into four pieces. Place the potato pieces in the boiling water and allow to boil for 20 minutes, until soft.

3. In the meantime, heat the oil in a large frying pan and fry the meat and onion until the meat is brown.

4. Add the vegetable soup and allow it to simmer for 15 minutes.

5. When the potatoes are soft, turn off the heat, drain them, and put them back in the saucepan. Add the milk and butter and mash until smooth (see page 47).

6. Place the meat mixture in a medium-sized ovenproof dish and spread the potato mash on top.

7. Run a fork along the mash to create lines and top with the grated cheese.

8. Bake in the oven for 20 minutes until golden brown.

Lamb Curry

| SERVES: 2 | PREPARATION TIME: 20 MINUTES | COOKING TIME: 30 MINUTES |

This Indian curry is delicious served with rice. You can add more heat, if you like, by adding chilies.

Ingredients

7 oz. (200 g) lean lamb, cubed
1 tablespoon vegetable oil
1 small onion
3.5 oz. (100 g) tikka masala curry paste
¾ cup (200 ml) natural yogurt
3 oz. (75g) basmati rice
small bunch fresh cilantro

1. Place the lamb in a saucepan with the oil. Set aside.

2. Peel and finely chop the onion. Add it to the lamb.

3. To cook the rice, heat ½ cup (125 ml) of water to boiling.

4. In the meantime, cook the lamb and onion over medium heat until the meat is brown.

5. Add the curry paste and stir well. Stir in the yogurt and allow to simmer for 30 minutes.

6. Add the rice to the boiling water and cook for about 20 minutes until all the water has been absorbed.

7. When the curry is cooked, sprinkle with cilantro leaves and serve with the rice.

Shish Kebabs

| SERVES: 4 | PREPARATION TIME: 20 MINUTES | COOKING TIME: 10 MINUTES |

This Turkish dish has been adopted the world over and is especially popular in Greece.

Ingredients

1¼ lb. (500 g) lean lamb, cubed
1 onion
2 oz. (50 g) red cabbage, sliced
2 tomatoes, sliced
4 pita breads
bunch fresh cilantro

For the marinade

3 tablespoons olive oil
juice 1 lemon
2 garlic cloves, peeled and chopped
salt and pepper

1. Mix all of the ingredients for the marinade in a bowl. Put the lamb into the marinade, cover the bowl with plastic wrap and leave it in the refrigerator for about 1 hour.

2. In the meantime, cut the onion into chunks and set aside.

3. When the meat is ready, divide the onion and meat into four equal portions. Thread each portion onto a metal skewer, starting with a piece of lamb, then some onion, then some lamb. Continue until it is all used up.

4. Place the skewers under a hot broiler for about 10 minutes, turning constantly, until the meat is cooked.

5. While the meat is cooking, toast the pita breads until they puff up. Slice them lengthwise to open.

6. Fill each pita bread with cabbage and tomato and serve with the warm kebabs.

Pork

Pork is a flavorful, nutritious meat that can be eaten in many ways. It is used to make many delicious foods such as sausages, ham, and bacon.

Raising Pigs

Contrary to what many people think, pigs are clean, intelligent animals. Traditionally they were raised in woodland areas, where they fed on acorns.

Today, most pigs are reared indoors. The animals are kept in groups in pens, but give birth in a separate farrowing house on individual farrowing crates. This is to protect the tiny piglets from being crushed by their supersized mom. The piglets leave the sow (female pig) after a month, and are then fed a carefully balanced diet so that they grow quickly and produce a lot of lean meat. Most pigs are slaughtered by the time they are six months old, when they weigh up to 220 pounds (100 kg).

Free-range pigs display natural instincts such as rooting in the soil. Because they are more active than indoor-reared pigs, they grow at a slower rate, so their meat becomes more flavorful and succulent.

Free Range Pigs

Some pigs are raised free range. Sturdier, fatter breeds are chosen for this because the animals must survive outdoors in all weathers. The sows are fed similar diets to animals kept indoors, but they also graze on grass. They need more food than indoor pigs because they use more energy roaming around. In summer, the pigs are given wallows of water to help them keep cool, as well as shade so that they are not burned by the sun. The pigs sleep in huts with straw bedding and give birth to their litters in individual shelters.

How Is Pork Eaten?

Fresh pork can be prepared in many different ways. The best cuts of meat can be roasted whole or thinly sliced and cooked in stir-fries. Fattier cuts of meat need gentle roasting or braising. Fresh pork can also be put through a grinder to provide ground pork. This can then be used in stuffings for vegetables or mixed with breadcrumbs, onions, herbs, and spices to make tasty meatballs. Turkeys cooked at Thanksgiving and Christmas are sometimes stuffed with a mixture of pork and herbs.

Fresh pork can also be processed. It is used in patés and to make sausages. It is also preserved as bacon and ham and is an ingredient in salami-type sausages, other lunchmeats, and pork pies. These preserved and processed meats were originally created as long lasting foods before refrigerators were invented. They are still popular because of their flavor, though we should avoid eating too many of them because they are often high in salt and fat.

Who Eats Pork?

Meat eaters all around the world eat pork, with the exception of Muslims and Jews, who consider pigs to be unclean. Pork is very popular in China, where it is added to stir-fries or used to make sweet and sour pork, soups, and spring rolls. In the UK, pork is traditionally served with apple sauce or enjoyed as bacon with eggs for breakfast. Other famous pork dishes include pork and beans, which is eaten in Brazil and Portugal, and sticky spareribs, which are eaten all over the United States. Hot dogs are a favorite food and are eaten almost everywhere in the world—most famously at baseball games. The traditional spicy frankfurter sausage is often made from a combination of meats, including beef and pork.

KNOW YOUR FOOD

If you are looking for lower-fat bacon, buy Canadian bacon instead of the regular kind.

 Hot dogs were one of the world's first "fast foods." They are served in a long bun, often with a helping of fried onions, mustard, or ketchup.

Cuts of Pork

Although pork is lighter in color than beef or lamb, it is still termed a red meat. As with beef and lamb, the animal's carcass is cut into different pieces, or cuts—big joints, lean fillets, chops, and so on. These cuts vary greatly and you can make the best of them by using different cooking methods. Almost every part of the pig can be eaten, including the feet, ears, and even the tail! The color of pork should be velvety mid-pink and the fat should be firm and white with skin that is dry and silky.

Loin, tenderloin, sirloin chops: These lean and tender cuts are suitable for broiling or frying. They also produce moist, tasty roasts. Sliced tenderloin and steaks are good for quick-cook stir-fries and kebabs.

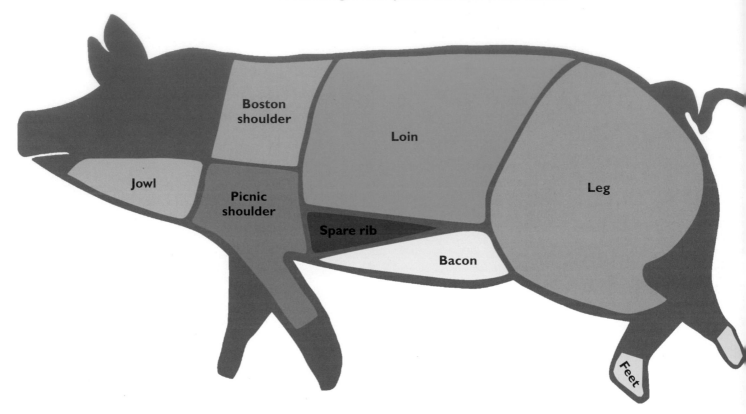

Boston shoulder

Loin

Jowl

Picnic shoulder

Leg

Spare rib

Bacon

Feet

Blade steak, picnic roast, spareribs: These flavorful, but fattier, cuts of meat are suitable for frying, gentle roasting, or braising. Spareribs are popular at barbecues and are easy to eat with your fingers.

KNOW YOUR FOOD

Before roasting, the layer of fat on the outside of pork can be scored with a sharp knife. It then cooks into a delicious, crunchy pork rind. Eat it only as a treat because it is very high in fat!

Sweet and Sour Pork

SERVES: 2	PREPARATION TIME: 20 MINUTES	COOKING TIME: 15–20 MINUTES

This dish is a wonderful mix of flavors. It is usually served with rice, but can be served with noodles, too.

Ingredients
11 oz. (300 g) lean pork
1 small piece fresh ginger
1 tablespoon vegetable oil
8 oz. (225 g) can pineapple chunks

For the sauce
2 tablespoons vinegar
1 tablespoon soy sauce
1 tablespoon tomato purée
1 tablespoon brown sugar
¾ cup (200 ml) cold water
1 level teaspoon cornstarch

1. Cut the pork into cubes. Cut the ginger as finely as possible.

2. Heat the oil in a saucepan over medium heat. Add the pork and ginger and cook until brown.

3. In the meantime, to make the sauce, mix all the sauce ingredients together.

4. When the meat is cooked, add the sauce and pineapple and stir well. Cook for 5 minutes.

5. Serve immediately.

COOK'S TIP

You can use chicken for this dish instead of pork.

Barbecue Spareribs

SERVES: 4	PREPARATION TIME: 20 MINUTES	COOKING TIME: 1 HOUR

These mouthwatering ribs are perfect for a summer barbecue served with a salad.

Ingredients
1 tablespoon vegetable oil
1 small onion, peeled and finely chopped
1 garlic clove, peeled and finely chopped
1½ lb. (675 g) spareribs
salad, to serve

For the sauce
2 tablespoons tomato purée
4 tablespoons cider vinegar
pinch chili powder
3 tablespoons honey
1 beef stock cube
½ cup (125 ml) water

1. Preheat the oven to 350°F (180°C).

2. Heat the oil in a frying pan over medium heat. Fry the onion and garlic until the onion changes color.

3. Add the sauce ingredients and stir well. Add a tablespoon more water if required. Cook for 10 minutes.

4. Use a pastry brush to spread the sauce all over the ribs.

5. Bake in the oven for 50 minutes, turning occasionally to ensure even cooking. Serve with a salad.

Danish Frikadeller (Meatballs)

SERVES: 2   PREPARATION TIME: 20 MINUTES   COOKING TIME: 12 MINUTES

This dish of meatballs is originally from Denmark. It is delicious served with boiled potatoes and cooked red cabbage.

Ingredients
1 small onion
1 garlic clove
9 oz. (250 g) ground pork
1 egg, beaten
1 tablespoon flour
1 tablespoon milk
2 tablespoons vegetable oil
salt and pepper
boiled potatoes, to serve
cooked red cabbage, to serve

1. Peel and finely chop the onion and garlic.

2. Put the onion, garlic, and all the other ingredients, except the oil, in a bowl. Squeeze them together with your hands to mix them well.

3. Roll the mixture into 6 equal balls and flatten each one to make an oval-shaped meatball.

4. Heat the oil in a large frying pan over medium heat. Add the meatballs and fry for 6 minutes. Turn them over and cook the other side for 6 minutes.

5. When cooked, remove the meatballs from the pan and place them on some paper towel to absorb any excess oil.

6. Serve with boiled potatoes and cooked red cabbage.

COOK'S TIP

These meatballs are great eaten cold in a sandwich.

Thai Pork with Orange

SERVES: 4   **PREPARATION TIME: 20 MINUTES**   **COOKING TIME: 15 MINUTES**

The citrus flavor from the oranges goes really well with the pork in this Thai recipe.

Ingredients
1 large orange
12 oz. (350 g) lean pork steak
1 tablespoon vegetable oil
1 garlic clove, peeled and finely chopped
3 tablespoons peanuts, finely chopped
1 tablespoon soy sauce
grated rind 1 orange
half teaspoon paprika
salt and pepper
lettuce leaves, to serve

1. Peel the orange, making sure you remove as much of the pith as possible. Cut the orange into segments.

2. Cut each segment into 2 pieces and set aside.

3. Remove any fat from the pork and cut it into strips.

4. Heat the oil over medium heat and fry the pork and garlic until lightly colored all over.

5. Stir in the peanuts and cook for 1 minute.

6. Add the remaining ingredients, except for the lettuce, and stir well.

7. To serve, put the pork on top of the lettuce leaves and pour the pan juices over the top.

COOK'S TIP

Lemon or lime can be used for a more tangy flavor.

29

Chicken and Other Poultry

Farmyard birds, such as chicken and turkey, are known as poultry. They are popular in everyday meals, as well as at celebrations, and are an excellent low-fat source of protein.

Breeding and Hatching

While some chickens are bred for their eggs, those chickens bred for their meat are known as broilers. Most farmers use fast-growing breeds that are strong and healthy and provide plenty of meat. The eggs are hatched in special hatcheries and the day-old chicks are then transported to rearing farms.

Indoors or Outdoors

The young birds are raised in different ways. Some are farmed intensively indoors in large, temperature-controlled houses. These conditions are highly specialized and result in the birds growing so quickly that they are ready to go to market in less than 40 days. Some people think that this kind of farming is cruel.

Free-range birds are raised outdoors, where they have access to light, and may have more room to flap their wings and scratch for food. Birds raised on the best poultry farms enjoy total freedom.

 These chickens are being raised intensively: indoors, in crowded conditions, and without natural light so that they are constantly feeding.

Food and Slaughter

The birds are fed on cereals mixed with soy and legumes. Some chickens have names that reflect their diet. For example, corn-fed chickens have yellow flesh and are widely considered to have more flavor than birds fed on soy. Intensively reared birds are slaughtered at about 5–6 weeks, free-range birds at about 8 weeks, and organic birds at about 10–11 weeks. After slaughter, the best birds are hung for several days, allowing their natural flavors to develop.

Turkeys are reared for about 20 weeks. Free-range and organic birds have a better taste because they are given more time to mature. Their meat is leaner and less fatty than an intensively reared bird.

FOOD FACTS

As a white meat, poultry is a healthy choice because it is lower in saturated fat than red meat. However, it does have fatty skin. The skin keeps the meat moist during cooking, but it is best to avoid eating it.

 Free-range turkeys can roam at will and are given plenty of time to grow. This produces a better tasting meat.

Processed Poultry

Chicken and turkey can be bought fresh or ready prepared. Some chicken meat is covered in breadcrumbs and sold as fried chicken, or kievs stuffed with garlic-flavored butter. Chicken "nuggets" are formed from cheaper meat and skin and can be high in fat. Chicken meat is also used in patés, pies, soups, and countless meals.

 A roast turkey with all the trimmings is the traditional Christmas dinner. Roast goose, a fattier meat, is sometimes eaten, too.

Who Eats Poultry?

Poultry is so easy to keep that it is raised and eaten all over the world. It is particularly popular in cultures that reject beef or pork. Famous chicken dishes include roast chicken, chicken soup, and chicken pie. In India, tandoori chicken and chicken tikka are popular, and chicken satay is eaten throughout Southeast Asia. Perhaps the world's most famous poultry dish is the roast turkey eaten for Thanksgiving Day in the U.S. and throughout the Christian world at Christmas.

Poultry Cuts

After slaughter, poultry birds are plucked, gutted, cleaned, and bagged. They are either sold whole or cut into portions. A whole bird is good value for money because it provides the basis for several meals. For example, a chicken can be roasted as part of a roast dinner, then the leftovers used in a stir-fry or salad. Finally, the carcass may be boiled with vegetables to make stock for a soup. Both turkey and chicken are available ground. This is a low-fat alternative to ground meat made from pork, lamb, or beef.

• Whole Birds

Whole birds can be roasted or boiled. Younger birds are more tender than older ones, so they are best for roasting. Older, tougher birds are better boiled. The meat can then be stripped and used in pies, stews, or soups.

FOOD FACTS

Chicken is the world's most popular meat. In the United States alone, 8,700,000,000 chickens are killed per year for consumption. Many people eat chicken up to three times a week.

• Chicken Portions

Pre-prepared portions of chicken and turkey are very convenient because they are small and cook more quickly than a whole bird. Only the best parts of the bird—the breasts, legs, and wings—are sold in this way.

• Breasts

The breast portions provide the most white meat. This meat is lean and very versatile. It can be eaten whole or cut into strips or cubes. Breast meat is good for kebabs or stir-fries. It does not have a lot of taste, but quickly takes on the flavor of other ingredients if you marinate or spice it before cooking.

• Legs

A leg can be bought as a single piece of meat or separated into the fleshier thigh and the narrow drumstick. Leg meat is darker, fattier, and more flavorful than breast meat. It can be roasted, broiled, poached, or fried. The thighs are also good for slower cooking. Drumsticks are often cooked on barbecues because they are easy to eat with your fingers.

• Wings

The wings contain little meat but they are delicious roasted or cooked on a barbecue. Wings should be eaten in moderation because they are high in fat.

KNOW YOUR FOOD

When buying poultry, choose a well-wrapped, undamaged bird with firm, plump flesh. It should have no smell whatsoever.

Buying a whole chicken is economical because it can be used to make several different meals. The best parts of the chicken are also sold as portions. They are: the breast (1); the wings (2), and the legs (3), which are sometimes called drumsticks.

Chicken Chop Suey

This Chinese dish is quick and easy and full of flavor. You can eat it with rice or noodles, or on its own.

Ingredients

1 boneless, skinless chicken breast
1 tablespoon vegetable oil
1 small cube fresh ginger
1 garlic clove
3 green onions
1 medium carrot
4 mushrooms
¼ napa cabbage
2 tablespoons soy sauce
3.5 oz. (100 g) bean sprouts

1. Cut the chicken breast into strips and place it in a wok with the oil. Set aside.

2. Prepare the garlic, ginger, and vegetables. Peel the garlic and ginger and chop them both finely.

3. Cut the dark green top off the green onions and slice the bulb.

4. Peel and slice the carrot into strips. Slice the mushrooms and chop the napa cabbage into narrow strips.

5. Fry the chicken with the soy sauce, garlic, and ginger until there is no pink meat left.

6. Add all the vegetables, including the bean sprouts, and cook for 5 minutes, stirring all the time. Serve immediately.

COOK'S TIP

You can add water chestnuts, bamboo shoots, or cashews for extra flavor and crunch.

Barbecue Drumsticks

| SERVES: 2 | PREPARATION TIME: 15 MINUTES | COOKING TIME: 20 MINUTES |

These drumsticks are delicious cooked under a broiler or on a barbecue.

Ingredients
4 chicken drumsticks
2 tablespoons ketchup
2 tablespoons light soy sauce
2 teaspoons honey
1 tablespoon vegetable oil
1 tablespoon lemon juice
½ teaspoon Chinese
   five spice powder
salad, to serve

1. Use a sharp knife to make 2–3 gashes on top of each drumstick.

2. Put the ketchup, soy sauce, honey, oil, lemon juice, and spice into a container and mix well.

3. Add the drumsticks, making sure they are coated in the marinade. Leave in the refrigerator for 2 hours.

4. Preheat the broiler on high heat. Place the chicken under the broiler, reserving the marinade. Lower the heat to medium and broil the chicken for 5 minutes.

5. Remove the chicken from the broiler and, using a pastry brush, coat the drumsticks with the marinade. Turn the drumsticks over to ensure even cooking. Return the chicken to the broiler for another 5 minutes before brushing and turning again. Broil for another 10 minutes.

6. Serve straight from the broiler with a side salad.

Malaysian Chicken

| SERVES: 4 | PREPARATION TIME: 30 MINUTES | COOKING TIME: 25–30 MINUTES |

The combination of fruit and chicken in a rich coconut sauce is irresistible. Serve this dish with plain boiled rice for a hearty main meal.

Ingredients
1 vegetable stock cube
1 cup (250 ml) boiling water
1 green bell pepper
1 red bell pepper
1 lb. (450 g) chicken meat (breast or thighs)
1 tablespoon vegetable oil
1 teaspoon ground cumin
1 teaspoon ground coriander
1 teaspoon turmeric
1 large onion, peeled and sliced
1 garlic clove, peeled and finely chopped
3 tablespoons coconut cream or coconut milk
9 oz. (250 g) pineapple, chopped

1. Mix the vegetable stock cube into the water and set aside.

2. Deseed and chop the peppers.

3. Cut the chicken into cubes.

4. Heat the oil over medium heat and add the spices, onion, garlic, chicken, and peppers. Fry for 2–3 minutes.

5. Add the stock, coconut cream, and pineapple, mix well, and heat to boiling. Turn down the heat and allow to simmer for 25 minutes. Serve in bowls.

Chicken Risotto

This recipe uses long-grain rice but Italians usually use arborio rice. They cook this until it is "al dente," which means slightly hard to bite.

Ingredients

2½ cups (625 ml) boiling water
1 chicken stock cube
1 garlic clove
1 boneless, skinless chicken breast
1 tablespoon vegetable oil
1 tablespoon soy sauce
1 small onion
3 oz. (75g) long-grain rice
2 oz. (50 g) frozen peas
2 oz. (50 g) frozen sweet corn

1. Add the stock cube to the boiling water and set aside.

2. Peel and finely chop the garlic. Set aside.

3. Cut the chicken into bite-sized cubes and put it into a large saucepan with the oil.

4. Add the garlic and soy sauce to the chicken and stir well.

5. Fry the chicken over medium heat until there is no pink left on it.

6. In the meantime, peel and finely chop the onion.

7. Add the rice and onion to the chicken and fry for 2 minutes. Add the stock to the chicken and stir well.

8. Add the peas and sweet corn to the chicken and cook on high until all the water has been absorbed. Serve piping hot.

COOK'S TIP

You can use turkey breasts instead of chicken breasts.

Turkey Breasts in Orange Sauce

SERVES: 4 | **PREPARATION TIME: 30 MINUTES** | **COOKING TIME: 40 MINUTES**

This turkey dish can also be served with rice or a side helping of carrots and green beans.

Ingredients

2 tablespoons black pepper
1 teaspoon dried oregano
2 garlic cloves, peeled and
  finely chopped
½ teaspoon ground cumin
½ cup (125 ml) orange
  juice
1 tablespoon honey
2 tablespoons olive oil
2¼ lb. (1 kg) skinless,
  boneless turkey breast
boiled new potatoes,
  to serve

1. Preheat the oven to 400°F (200°C).

2. To make a marinade, mix the pepper, oregano, garlic, cumin, orange juice, honey, and oil together to make a paste.

3. Put the turkey breasts in a bowl and pour the marinade over them. Cover with plastic wrap and leave in the refrigerator for 10 minutes.

4. Take the turkey out of the marinade and place it on a baking sheet. Bake for 25 minutes.

5. Place the remaining marinade in a saucepan and allow it to simmer until reduced.

6. When the turkey is cooked, cut each breast into thick slices, pour the sauce over, and serve with the potatoes.

Chicken Soup

SERVES: 4 | **PREPARATION TIME: 25 MINUTES** | **COOKING TIME: 35–40 MINUTES**

The combination of chicken and pasta makes this a delicious, hearty soup—perfect for a winter's day.

Ingredients

2½ cups (625 ml) boiling water
half an uncooked chicken
1 small onion, peeled and
  finely chopped
2 carrots, peeled and diced
2 sticks celery, chopped
1 vegetable stock cube
3.5 oz. (100 g) dried pasta
1 tablespoon butter
salt and pepper

1. Put the water into a large saucepan and heat to boiling.

2. Add the chicken to the boiling water, with the onion, carrots, and celery, and boil for 20 minutes.

3. Remove the chicken from the water, allowing the soup to simmer.

4. Remove the skin and bones from the chicken and cut up the meat into small pieces. Return the meat to the soup.

5. Add the stock cube, pasta, and butter and heat to boiling. Turn down the heat and allow the soup to simmer for 20 minutes. Check that there is enough liquid in the soup, adding more as it cooks, if required.

6. Season to taste and serve.

Fish and Shellfish

A huge variety of animals live in the sea—from giant tuna to tiny sprats and shrimps. They make light, quick, healthy meals and are a prime source of quality protein.

How and Where Are Fish Caught?

Fish are caught all over the world, in freshwater rivers and lakes and in the sea. Fishing is tough, sometimes dangerous, work. Some fishing boats are small and stay close to the coast, using nets and lines. The fish are gutted by hand on board, packed in ice, and brought back to market. Then they are sold by auction.

Other fishing boats are like floating factories, remaining at sea for several weeks. They use enormous nets to trawl the seabed. The huge catch is gutted and frozen before the boats reach land, where the fish is sold at market.

Fish Farming

As wild fish stocks are declining, there has been a growth in fish farming (aquaculture). About one-third of seafood is currently produced by fish farms. Fish such as salmon, sea bass, cod, and halibut are raised in hatcheries and then reared in cages in the sea. Trout are raised in tanks near rivers.

Shellfish farms include shrimp raised in estuaries in tropical waters and mussels reared on ropes attached to rafts. Other species farmed in some countries include oysters, scallops, and clams.

 This huge catch of pollock has been pulled up by trawlers in the Bering Sea, off the coast of Alaska. With many fish species at dangerously low levels, fish farming is a growing industry.

Conserving Stocks

There are certain times in the year when you cannot buy a particular kind of fish unless it is frozen. Fish need to breed or they will die out. When they are ready to lay their eggs, female fish have thousands of tiny eggs called roe in their bodies. If they are caught before they have had time to release the eggs into the sea, then there will be no new fish and the numbers of fish in the sea will be fewer.

Preserving Fish

Fish is a highly perishable food, but it can be preserved in a number of ways, including freezing, salting, pickling, smoking, and canning.

- In salting, the fish is packed in layers of salt until all of the liquid has drained off. Salt cod is very popular in Spain.
- In pickling, fish is soaked in vinegar and herbs. Scandinavian fresh herring fillets are preserved in this way and are known as rollmops.

FOOD FACTS

Fresh and frozen tuna and other oily fish is rich in Omega-3 and -6 oils, which are important for healthy hearts and digestion. We should try to eat one portion of oily fish a week.

- Smoking fish improves its flavor and texture. Some smoked fish, such as smoked herring, needs cooking. Others, such as salmon or mackerel, do not.
- Canning suits oily fish, such as tuna, as well as seafood, such as crab. Anchovies are filleted, salted, and packed in oil. Salmon, sardines, and tuna are canned in brine, spring water, oil, or tomato sauce.

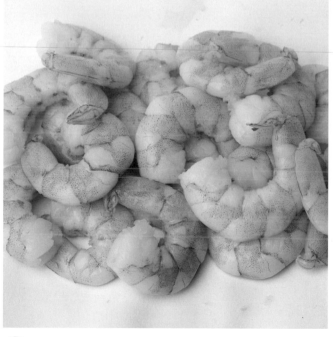

Raw shrimp, when shelled, are gray in color (left). The flesh turns a pale pink when the shrimp are cooked (right).

Who Eats Fish?

Fish is eaten all over the world, particularly in coastal areas and near rivers and lakes. The world's greatest fish eaters are the Japanese, who eat fish nearly every day. Fish is also very popular in Iceland, Scandinavia, and countries around the Mediterranean Sea.

Famous fish dishes include fish and french fries, which is eaten in the UK, a fish soup called chowder, which is popular in the United States, and a stew called bouillabaisse, which is eaten in France. In Spain, a fish-and-rice dish called paella is popular and in the Far East, fish curry is regularly made.

Buying Fish

Because fish perishes easily, it has to be transported quickly in refrigerated trains and trucks. In stores, it is usually displayed on a bed of crushed ice to keep it chilled. All fresh fish must be eaten promptly on the day you buy it. Ideally, it should be eaten within two or three days of being caught.

When buying fish, choose fresh-looking, moist, shiny fish with bright eyes, firm flesh, and a clean smell. Smoked fish should look glossy. If buying prepacked fish, always check the use-by date.

Fish and french fries is a traditional English dish. It is at its best when eaten on the coast, where the fish is always fresh.

This display of fresh fish and shellfish includes salmon, tuna, flounder, scallops, and oysters. The food is displayed on a bed of crushed ice, in order to preserve it.

Fish Cuts

Fresh fish is usually sold whole. Larger species, such as cod and salmon, are also cut up and sold in fillets or steaks. All fish, whether whole or in pieces, can be poached, steamed, broiled, fried, or roasted in the oven. Fish can also be used to make soups, fish cakes, stews, and pies. A lot of fish and shellfish is sold frozen. This is convenient because it has usually been cleaned and so there is no or little waste.

• Whole Fish

Whole fish are cleaned by gutting—in other words, they are slit open and all the inner organs are removed. The head may also be removed. The fish are then washed under running water. The bones and organs in a fish can amount to more than half of its weight.

• Fillets

In a filleted fish, the flesh has been taken off the bones. This results in long, thin pieces that are easy to eat and can be cooked very quickly.

• Steaks

Steaks are slices of whole fish, usually cut across the bone. The thicker the steak, the longer it will take to cook.

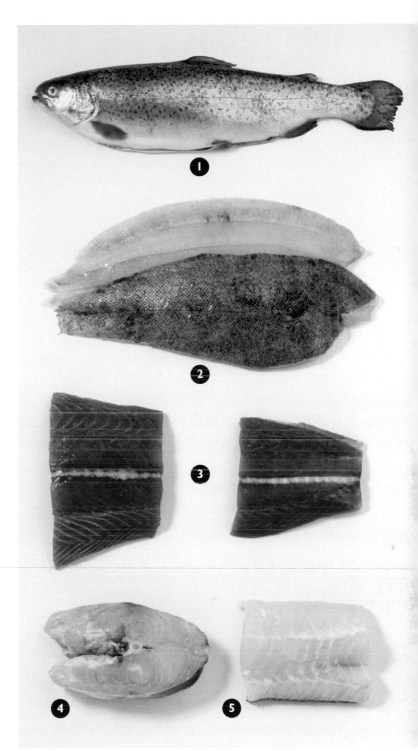

 Fish can be eaten whole on the bone or in smaller portions such as fillets and steaks. From top:
1 Whole trout
2 Fillets of sole
3 Sliced salmon fillets
4 Cod steak
5 Haddock fillet

FOOD FACTS

Nutritionists recommend that we eat two portions of fish a week, one of which should be oil-rich.
Here are some examples of a portion of fish:
1 medium-sized fillet of white fish
1 medium-sized fresh mackerel
1 drained can of tuna or salmon
6 fish fingers
2 small cans of mackerel or sardines

Garlic Shrimp

SERVES: 2 | PREPARATION TIME: 5 MINUTES | COOKING TIME: 10 MINUTES

This dish makes a great appetizer—it is full of flavor but light enough to get your tastebuds going before a main meal.

Ingredients
2 garlic cloves, peeled and
    finely chopped
1 tablespoon butter
10 uncooked shrimp
1 tablespoon parsley, chopped

1. Place the butter, garlic, and shrimp in a frying pan and cook over medium heat for four minutes on each side. The shrimp will turn light pink when cooked.

2. Remove the pan from the heat, add the chopped parsley, and stir well.

3. Serve the shrimp in glass bowls.

Tuna Steaks and Couscous

SERVES: 2 | PREPARATION TIME: 10 MINUTES | COOKING TIME: 7–10 MINUTES

Couscous salad goes well with fish because it is light but full of flavor.

Ingredients
juice 1 lime
1 tablespoon soy sauce
2 garlic cloves, peeled and
    finely chopped
2 fresh tuna steaks
1 tablespoon oil

For the couscous
1 cup (175 g) couscous
1 small onion, peeled and
    finely chopped
2 tomatoes, chopped small
1 small bunch fresh cilantro,
    chopped

1. Mix the lime juice, soy sauce, and chopped garlic in a large bowl.

2. Place the tuna steaks in the bowl and coat with the sauce.

3. Heat the oil in a frying pan, then cook the tuna for 3–4 minutes on each side.

4. In the meantime, put the couscous in a large bowl and cover with boiling water. Add the onions, tomatoes, and cilantro to the bowl.

5. When the tuna is cooked, halve the couscous and serve with the tuna steaks on top.

Fish Cakes

MAKES: 4 **PREPARATION TIME: 30 MINUTES** **COOKING TIME: 35 MINUTES**

These fish cakes are perfect for dipping in sweet chili sauce as an appetizer, or serve them with a summer salad as a main meal.

Ingredients
1 tablespoon butter
3.5 oz. (100 g) fresh cod
2 medium potatoes
1 tablespoon chopped parsley
2 eggs, beaten
salt and pepper
2 oz. (50 g) breadcrumbs
sweet chili sauce, to serve

1. Preheat the oven to 400°F (200°C).

2. Half fill a medium saucepan with water and place it over high heat to boil.

3. In the meantime, place one-third of the butter on a large sheet of foil and lay the fish on top. Add 2 tablespoons of water and fold the foil around the cod to make a parcel. Place the parcel on a baking sheet and bake for 15 minutes.

4. While the fish is cooking, peel and cut the potatoes into 4 and add them to the boiling water. Allow to cook for 20 minutes.

5. When the fish is cooked, carefully remove it from the foil and flake it into pieces in a mixing bowl. Leave the oven on.

6. Drain the potatoes, return them to the pan, and add the remaining butter. Mash until smooth (see page 47).

7. Add the mashed potatoes to the fish with the parsley, half the egg, salt, and pepper and mix well.

8. Use your hands to shape the mixture into 4 fish cakes.

9. Dip each fish cake in the remaining egg, then coat it in the breadcrumbs.

10. Bake in the oven for 15 minutes until golden. Serve with the sweet chili sauce.

COOK'S TIP

Try using tuna or salmon for a different flavor.

Fish Pot Pie

To serve more people, double this recipe and use a larger ovenproof dish.

Ingredients
3.5 oz. (100 g) salmon fillet
3.5 oz. (100 g) white fish
1 tablespoon lemon juice
salt and pepper
3.5 oz. (100 g) ready-made puff pastry
peas, to serve

For the sauce
2 tablespoons (30 g) butter
¼ cup (25 g) flour, extra for dusting
1¼ cups (300 ml) milk

1. Preheat the oven to 350°F (180°C).

2. To make the sauce, heat the butter in a saucepan over medium heat. Stir in the flour and use a wooden spoon to mix well to make a smooth paste.

3. Slowly add the milk, stirring constantly until the sauce thickens and coats the back of the wooden spoon. Turn the heat down low and allow to simmer.

4. Remove any skin from the fish and cut it into cubes. Add the lemon juice and mix well.

5. Add the cubed fish to the white sauce and season to taste. Stir well and remove from the heat.

6. On a floured work surface, roll out the pastry to a slightly larger shape than the ovenproof dish.

7. Place the fish and sauce in the dish and cover with the rolled pastry. Trim around the edges of the dish to remove any excess pastry. Brush the pastry with a little milk.

8. Bake the pot pie in the oven for 20 minutes until golden. Serve with cooked peas.

COOK'S TIP

If you do not like salmon, you can replace it with any white fish.

Thai Shrimp Curry

| SERVES: 4 | PREPARATION TIME: 10 MINUTES | COOKING TIME: 10 MINUTES |

With a cooking time of about 10 minutes, this is quick and easy food at its best!

Ingredients
1 tablespoon vegetable oil
1¼ lb. (500 g) cooked bay shrimp
1 onion, peeled and finely chopped
1 garlic clove, peeled and finely chopped
2 teaspoons Thai green curry paste
¾ cup (200 ml) coconut milk

1. Heat the oil in a wok over medium heat.

2. Add the bay shrimp, onion, garlic, and curry paste and fry for 3 minutes.

3. Add the coconut milk and cook for a further 5 minutes. Serve hot.

Spinach and Fish Bake

| SERVES: 4 | PREPARATION TIME: 30 MINUTES | COOKING TIME: 40 MINUTES |

This fish bake is full of flavor. You can use a combination of fish, for example, cod and salmon.

Ingredients
1¼ lb. (500 g) potatoes, peeled
1¼ lb. (500 g) any fresh uncooked fish
1 lb. (450 g) spinach
1 tablespoon butter
2 tablespoons milk
9 oz. (250 g) sour cream
2 oz. (50 g) Cheddar cheese, grated

1. Half fill a large saucepan with water and heat to boiling.

2. Cut the potatoes into quarters. Add them to the boiling water and cook on high until the potatoes are soft.

3. Preheat oven to 350°F (180°C).

4. Remove any skin from the fish and cut it into cubes.

5. Cook the spinach in a large pan for 2 minutes—it is not necessary to add oil to the pan.

6. When the potatoes are soft, take them off the heat and mash them with the butter and milk.

7. Place the fish in an ovenproof dish. Cover it with the sour cream and the spinach before topping with the mashed potato.

8. Sprinkle the pie with the grated cheese and bake for 30–40 minutes until the cheese is golden.

45

Glossary

aquaculture	using the sea, lakes, and rivers to raise fish and shellfish		**perishable**	likely to rot or spoil quickly
bacteria	tiny living organisms; some are helpful in the body, and others can be harmful		**pesticide**	a chemical substance that is used to kill pests or weeds
braising	cooking slowly with a small amount of liquid in a closed dish		**pith**	the white tissue than lines the skin of citrus fruits
carcass	the dead body of an animal		**poached**	simmered in a liquid
couscous	a North African dish of crushed wheat		**pot-roasting**	braising meat and vegetables with a little water in a covered pot
cured	preserved		**preservative**	a chemical substance that is added to food to make it last longer
escalope	a thin slice of boneless meat		**preserve**	to make food last longer by adding chemicals or using methods such as salting, pickling, or smoking
farrowing house	the place where a sow gives birth to piglets		**processed food**	treated or pre-prepared food
fiber	the bulky part of food that is needed for digestion		**protein**	a nutrient that helps the body to grow and repair itself
fillet	a boneless piece of meat or fish		**saturated fat**	a type of fat that is harmful to the body because it builds up in the arteries and causes heart disease
free range	raised outdoors		**simmering**	to gently boil
grain	the seed that comes from edible grasses, such as rice and oats		**species**	a particular kind of animal
ham	cured meat from the leg of a pig		**tandoori**	cooked on a spit over charcoal in a clay oven
intensive farming	raising a large number of animals in a small space		**tikka**	marinated in yogurt and spices and cooked in a clay oven
legumes	pod-bearing plants such as beans, the seeds of which can be dried and used as food		**trotter**	a pig's foot used as food
litter	a group of young animals, born at the same time from the same mother		**vitamin**	a special substance found in food that the body needs in tiny amounts to stay healthy
livestock	farm animals, such as cattle, pigs, and poultry			
marinated	soaked in a liquid mixture to add flavor			
mineral	a substance, such as iron, that is found in the soil and the foods we eat			
nutrient	any part of a food that gives the body energy or the goodness it needs to grow			
organic	raised without the use of chemicals such as antibiotics, pesticides, or preservatives			
paté	a spread made from chopped meat or fish and blended with herbs and spices			

Food Safety

Sticking to some simple rules can help you avoid food poisoning and other kitchen dangers.

1. Clean all your work surfaces before you start cooking.

2. If you have long hair, tie it back away from your face.

3. To avoid a serious injury, always wear shoes in the kitchen.

4. Wash your hands well with soap and warm water before you start to cook. Wash them after handling any raw meat, poultry, or fish.

5. Read through the recipe you are cooking before you start. Check that you have all the equipment and ingredients that you will need.

6. Check the use-by dates on all food.

7. Wash all fruit and vegetables under cold, running water.

8. When preparing food, keep it out of the refrigerator for the shortest time possible. Generally, you should not leave food out for longer than 2 hours.

9. Use a different cutting board and knife to prepare meat, chicken, and fish from the one you use for preparing fruit and vegetables.

10. Never serve undercooked food, ensure that any meat, fish, and chicken is cooked all the way through.

11. Replace used dish towels regularly with clean, dry ones to avoid the spreading of bacteria.

Useful Techniques

Dicing
Cut the meat, fruit or vegetable intro strips about ½ inch (1 centimeter) wide, then chop to give you cubes about ½ inch (1 centimeter) in size.

Mashing
Use either a fork or a masher to press down to squash the fruit or vegetable. Continue to do this until there are no lumps left.

Blanching
Place the vegetables in a saucepan with just enough boiling water to cover them. Keep them in the water for the required time, which will vary depending on the recipe.

Peeling Tomatoes
Use a sharp knife to make a cross at the bottom of the tomato. Cover the tomato with boiling water and leave to stand for 3 minutes before removing. The skin should peel back from the cross.

Tenderizing
Place the meat on a chopping board and, using a meat tenderizer, hit the meat on each side.

Spicing
Place the meat on a chopping board. Using your preferred spices, massage them in to the cut of meat.

KNOW YOUR FOOD

Useful information
These abbreviations have been used:
lb.—pound   **oz.**—ounce
ml—milliliter   **l**—liter
g—gram   **kg**—kilogram

1 teaspoon = 5 milliliters
1 tablespoon = 15 milliliters

All eggs are medium unless stated.

Cooking temperatures:
To figure out where the stove dial needs to be for high, medium, and low heat, count the marks on the dial and divide them by three. The top few are high, the bottom few are low, and the in-between ones are medium.

Index

Further Reading

Body Fuel For Healthy Bodies: Meats, Fish, Eggs, Nuts, and Beans
by Trisha Sertori (Marshall Cavendish Children's Books, 2008)

Fish, Meat, and Poultry: Dangers in the Food Supply
by Daniel E. Harmon (Rosen Central, 2008)

Meat, Fish, and Eggs
by Susan Martineau and Hel James (Smart Apple Media, 2009)

Web Sites

Due to the changing nature of Internet links, Rosen Publishing has developed an online list of Web sites related to the subject of this book. This site is regularly updated. Please use this link to access this list: http://www.rosenlinks.com/cook/cmf